Travel In Enjoying India To The Fullest

Things to do in India

By

Shalu Sharma

Copyright:

Copyright © 2015 Shalu Sharma. All Rights Reserved.

http://www.shalusharma.com

No portion of this book may be modified, reproduced or distributed mechanically, electronically or by any other means including photocopying without the written permission of the author.

Disclaimer:

Whilst every care is taken to ensure that the information in this book is as up-to-date and accurate as possible, no responsibility can be taken by the author for any errors or omissions contained herein. Responsibility for any loss, damage, accident or distress resulting from adherence to any advice, suggestions or recommendations is not taken.

Other books by the author:

Essential India Travel Guide: Travel Tips And Practical Information

India Travel Health Guide: Health Advice and Tips for Travelers to India

Travel Delhi: Places to Visit in Delhi

India Travel Survival Guide For Women

Essential Hindi Words And Phrases For Travelers To India

Hinduism For Kids: Beliefs And Practices

India For Kids: Amazing Facts About India

Hindi Language For Kids And Beginners: Speak Hindi Instantly

Real Ghost And Paranormal Stories From India

Introduction

India is not just about site seeing, it's about experiencing it! Unless you try some of the interesting things India has to offer then your trip to India will be pretty much useless. There is no point hopping from one monument to another without actually doing some of the things India is all about. So why not roll up your sleeves and get your hands dirty and do exactly what Indians do. If you are travelling to India and want to get the most of your trip to India then this is the book for you.

Those who have not visited India before, they will find the place hot, noisy, dusty and outright weird and would never want to come back. But there are many who keep coming back to India because they have fallen in love with the place. Many of you would have heard lots of things about India particularly its backwardness, crimes against women, beggars on the streets, poverty and so on. But there is no denying that it is one of the fastest growing economies of the world and the West is looking at India for business. You have to come, feel and experience some of the things India is all about.

If you want to enjoy the real India and its many layers of beauty and wonder then you will need to capture it by doing some of the things mentioned in this book. If you are thinking that by coming to this country, you will enjoy yourself and will have a relaxing holiday then you are mistaken, in fact you will be disappointed. But if you come to India with an open mind to see what India is all about then that it is where all the magic will begin – that is when you will start really enjoying India.

Please note that this is not a travel guide but a list of interesting things which are unique to India that you can do on your trip. Tourists from all around the world are coming to India and going back without actually experiencing the real India. It is a wasted opportunity for some. This book gives you a list of things you can do and enjoy in India. For tips and travel guide you can visit ShaluSharma.com.

Drink Indian chai

One of the best things you can do in India is to have a cup of Indian chai (tea) at one of the roadside stalls. These are completely safe to drink. To those coming from Europe and USA, the Indian chai will taste completely different. What gives the Indian chai a distinct taste is the smell of leaves and milk that has been extensively boiled. Unlike in the west where the tea is made by dipping tea bags in boiled water with a dash of cold milk, the tea here is made by boiling water, milk, loose tea leaves and sugar. The tea is kept boiling on a coal fire. Just try it, you know never know you might like it. It only costs a few rupees.

The Indian chai on the roadside – A must try in India

Sit on a rickshaw and take a ride

Rickshaws are a part of life in many parts of India including Old Delhi. It may seem odd to be pulled manually by a man but it is a source of income for millions of rickshaw pullers. Feel free to hire one of these rickshaws. They are best for short distances. Make sure you fix the price before you get on one of these rickshaws. Whatever you do, don't ride one without fixing the fare otherwise you might get overcharged. If you do feel pity for the man, then feel free to give him a tip.

Ride a rickshaw – make sure you fix the price first

Drink cold coffee

Some tourists have said that coffee tastes much better in India. This is perhaps all down to the taste of the ground water. There are numerous shops and stalls everywhere where you could try cold coffee. This particular one is at Janpath Market in Connaught Place are of New Delhi. Just ask for a bottle of cold coffee and try it. I am sure coffee lovers will like it.

Drink cold coffee at the numerous stalls and outlets in the market place

Visit an Indian home

If you are visiting India to experience the Indian culture then one of the best ways to understand the people and culture is by visiting an Indian home. It might be difficult to visit an Indian home if you don't know anyone in India. But if you have an Indian friend or know anyone Indian in your own country then you can ask them if you could visit their home. If you are visiting an Indian home for the first then here are some tips on my website. Here's the URL: http://www.shalusharma.com/visiting-an-indian-home

Whatever you do, don't talk politics. Politics is a hot topic and can often get out of control.

Get to learn about Indian culture by visiting an Indian home

Get your horoscope prepared

India is hot on horoscopes. Every child born in India has a horoscope. These horoscopes are based on planetary positions when the child was born and is supposed to explain all the future events in the life of the child. Although these horoscopes are not meant to be taken seriously but it gives a kind of idea about what the child will do their life and if there are any mishaps then it could be avoided. You can get a horoscope for about 500 rupees at any temple. Some temples have special counters where you can get your horoscope. They are mainly in Hindi or the local language. You can always get it translated if you find a translator there and then or bring it back home and then find one the net.

Some temples can prepare horoscopes for you

Have your hand read by an astrologer

Having your hand read is another favourite pastime for the Indians. Astrology is big business and you will find lots of people sitting on the roadside especially at temples who will read your palm and tell you about your future. Whatever you do, don't take it seriously and don't get into a trap where the astrologer asks you to buy something.

Have your hand read by an astrologer. You never know, you might discover something

Eat at the roadside

If you love Indian food then you are going to love India, in fact you can enjoy the real Indian food compared to what you have been used. The street food of India has its own attraction. There are many types of street food from the humble "chaat" to "pav bhaji". You have to be a little cautious but there are no reasons not to try these street foods if you have water borne diseases jabs before you come to India. Here's a street food guide: http://www.shalusharma.com/indian-street-food

Try some of the street snacks

See a Hindi movie at the theatres

India is the largest movie producing country in the world. Why not spend an evening watching an Indian movie. There are wonderful multiplexes in the major cities - just ask your hotel which one. Remember, Indian movies are quite long and you might get bored. But if you are feeling up for the challenge then certainly try one. You never know, you might like it. But if you are a movie fanatic then you should definitely watch a Hindi in India.

Watch an Indian movie at the theatres

Drink Lassi

Lassi is a very popular drink in India made of yogurt, milk, Indian spices and often with fruits. It is a bit like the smoothie or milk shake. The ingredients are mixed and churned together to make the lassi. It is very popular in the summer months as it is supposed to have a cooling effect. There are several types of lassi – sweet lassi, salty lassi, mango lassi and the bhang lassi. The bhang lassi is the marijuana milk shakes available in the holy city of Varanasi. The other types of lassi are available in most restaurants and street vendors sell them too.

Drink a glass of lassi, the traditional Indian drink

Travel to Agra and return the same day on a train

Agra in the state of Uttar Pradesh is where the Taj Mahal is situated. If you are in Delhi then you can hire a car and visit Agra. Your hotel should be able to arrange you a car. It takes about 4 to 5 hours to get and if you set off at 6 or 7 in the morning then you will have enough time explore the Taj Mahal. You can always take the early train from New Delhi Railway Station (at 6 am) to Agra and come back the same day. It takes about 1 and half hours. This will give you enough time to get to the Taj Mahal and even explore Agra Fort and return back to New Delhi.

Visit the Taj Mahal and go back to Delhi the same day

Buy some Indian clothes

Indians love wearing bright clothes particularly Indian women. You will see women wearing colourful "sarees" or "salwar kameez". Why not buy some of these to take back home with you. Wearing the saree is quite tricky but the salwar kameez is pretty easy enough and you can spend your entire holiday in these clothes. Here's how to wear the saree: http://www.shalusharma.com/how-to-wear-saree

The Indian shawl is another piece of clothing you can buy. There are plenty of shops from street vendors to large malls where you can buy them. Men can buy "kurta pajamas" a bit like the western sleeping dress.

Buy Indian clothes. Don't be afraid to ask and get them out. Choose something that you like

Get an Indian oil massage

Treat yourself to oil massage in India. Who doesn't like lying down and having a relaxing massage? So why not get one of these. The Ayurvedic sarvangadhara is popular one to go for. It is a form of complete body massage that uses especially formulated herbal oil which is poured all over the body while massaging rhythmical. These types of massages are brilliant for the relief of muscular pain. You will have to find a massage parlour or a spa. You hotel should be able to direct you to a good one. Make sure they are of good repute.

Have an oil massage in India

Buy some Indian jewellery

India is big on jewellery and when Indians buy them, they go for the real thing – 22 to 24 carat gold. You will find jewellery shops everyone. There are smaller shops but I suggest you keep away from them unless you are a trader and know what you are going. But if you aren't sure then stick with silver which are cheaper. One particular item you can buy is the "payal" or anklets which are worn in the legs.

Ladies might want to buy some bangles to take back home

Eat Indian sweets

India is country of sweet lovers. Those who love sweet things then you must try Indian sweets. Some of the Indian street foods include rasmalai, ragulla, jelabi, peda and so on. You can order them at the restaurant or you can buy them at a local sweet shop just like you would in a bakery.

A sweet shop selling varieties of Indian sweets. Just try them

Chew Paan

Paan is betel leaf stuffed with paan masala. You can chew paan in local paan shops that you will find on the roads. There are different types of paan and some will have tobacco. If you don't like tobacco then try the sweet one. The ones with the tobacco is called "jarda paan" while the ones that are sweet is called "meetha paan". The ingredients in the betel leaf are tobacco, lime, sweetened coconut, spices, mint and other paan masala. Here's more on the paan: http://www.shalusharma.com/try-chewing-paan-in-india

Chances are that you will not like this but it's worth a try. It does not cost more than 20 Rupees per paan.

Paan ingredients at a paan shop

Drink juice on the side of the road

You will find juice stalls at the road side. Drinking fresh juices will keep you hydrated and keep you going. You will find all sorts of juices being sold. Some of the popular ones include oranges and sugarcanes. Just make sure that there is nothing in the container when it's being prepared. You can have them squeezed in your own mug if you like.

Drink freshly squeezed fruit juices at the road side stalls

Get entertained by a street vendor

There is no denying that India is still a developing country and many people make their living by selling things on the road particular at the tourist locations. In fact, no matter where you go, there will be street vendors or touts. Some of these vendors have really good things. For instance this one in the picture was selling needles that make sewing a breeze. I had never seen something like this before so I bought two of them at 100 rupees for a pair. So if you do see something interesting then feel free to check it out. Here are some bargaining tips: http://www.shalusharma.com/how-to-bargain-in-india

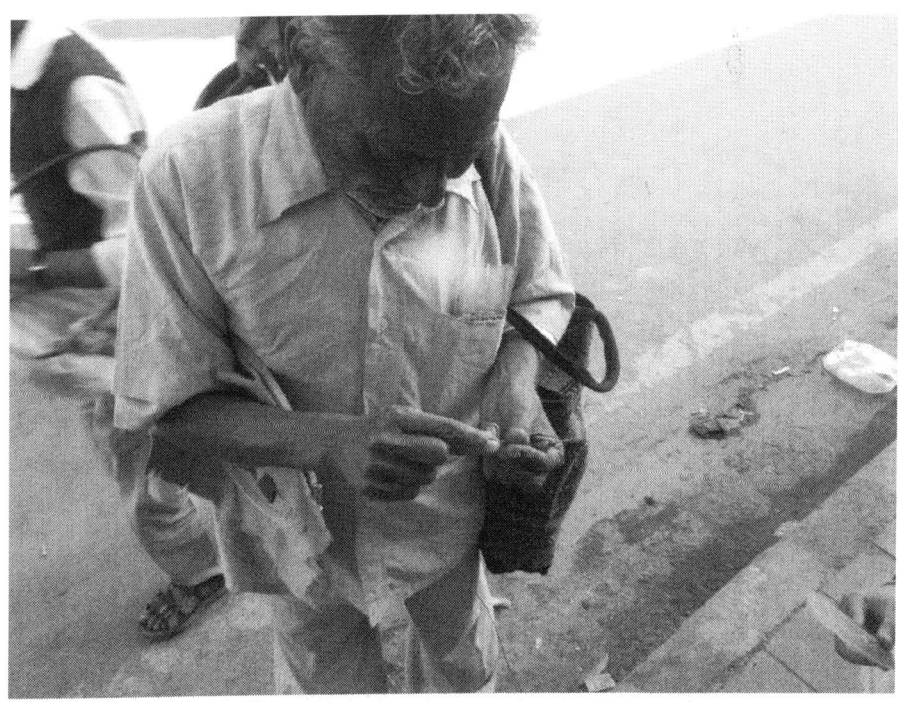

A tout selling fancy needles. Bought 2 of these

Get your boot polished

It is a slightly unusual thing but boot polishing on the streets is still prevalent in India. Lots of Indian people have their boots polished on the go. You will find boot polishers coming up to you who will offer to polish your boots. Sad it may be but many people make a living like this. Why not have your shoes polished and even repaired for a fraction of the cost compared to your own country. This shouldn't cost you more than a few rupees (around 20 or 50). Most of the boot polishers can be seen around market places, railway and bus stations.

Get your leather shoes polished and repaired

Take part in Indian festivals

India is called the land of festivals. Some of the popular festivals include Holi (festivals of colours), Diwali (festivals of light) and Durga Puja (worship of Goddess Durga). Holi is celebrated around March. Some hotels organise Holi festival for their guests. As for Diwali, just take a walk around the evening and get entertained by the display of lights and fireworks. You just have to time your holiday around these festivals.

Celebrate Indian festivals

Buy books

Books are cheaper in India compared to the West as production costs are cheaper. So why not buy some books. No matter what you are interested in, you should be able to buy all sorts of books from Medical books to fiction. There are plenty of book shops in every market. If you can't find a book, just asks the person at the counter, they might have it in their storage and will get you the desired book if they have it.

Books are cheaper in India

Visit a temple and offer your prayers

India is a very religious place and you will find temples everywhere. Some of the popular temples of Delhi include the Akshardham, Birla Temple, ISKCON Temple Delhi, Hanuman Temple in Connaught Place and the Shani Dham Temple. Some will allow you to buy offerings which you can give to the priest who will do a prayer on your behalf. No matter where you are, just visit a local temple and offer your prayers. Here are some basics of the Hindu religion: http://www.shalusharma.com/hinduism-facts

Visit a temple and offer your prayers. You never know, your wishes might come true

Go for a Yoga course

If you are a yoga fan then why not do a course or go to a yoga retreat right here in India where it all began. You can also buy some yoga CDs to bring back home. The popular yoga videos of Baba Ramdev are available in most book shops. Rishikesh (in Uttarakhand state) located in the foothills of the Himalayas has lots of yoga retreats you can go for. Some of the retreats have courses for beginners.

Learn some yoga at the numerous yoga retreats

Take a dip in the Ganges and wash your sins away

If you happen to be visit Varanasi, one of the most holy place for the Hindus then why not visit one of the numerous ghats and take a dip in the River Ganges just like the locals do. It is said that your sins will wash away. You do have to make a pledge that you will not commit any sins otherwise taking a dip will be useless. It's an experience you will not forget.

Take a dip in the Ganges to wash your sins away

Give money to beggars

One of the sad realities of India is that there are beggars on the streets. Although poverty has been eliminated to a very large extent but beggars continue to exist. If you are feeling sorry for them then you could give a few rupees to the beggars. Many of these beggars will appear from nowhere. If you are in a taxi or an auto-rickshaw then some will just pop up when the vehicle stops at the traffic lights. Just keep some change handy and give it to them.

Give some money to the beggars

Get entertained by monkey tricks

In smaller towns, you will find entertainers doing tricks with animals. The one my children love is the monkey show. They are a lot of fun and these monkeys are really something, they can do a lot of tricks and sure to entertain you and the family for a while. The entertainers will expect a few rupees in return. It will all depend where you are going. There are plenty of these in the city of Agra (where the Taj Mahal is).

Get entertained by monkeys. Children will love them

Take a tea tour in Darjeeling

India is one of the largest producers of tea and most of the tea drank by people in the West comes from India. If you love tea then why not organise to go on a tea tour in the tea gardens of Darjeeling. There are about 80 tea gardens in Darjeeling and you could organise yourself a visit. Just mind you, these tours might be a little expensive but if you can afford it, it's worth doing it. So why not walk and enjoy the tea gardens of India. But remember, tea tourism is not an organised sector and you will have to find out how to visit the gardens yourself. Your hotel could do that for you.

Take a tea tour and go on a mountain train

Visit a Gurdwara and have food at the langar

The place of worship of the Sikhs is called a Gurdwara. It is very similar to the Hindu temples but you will not find any statues of Gods and Goddesses. Just like all temples and places of worship in India, you will have to take your shoes off and cover your head with a cloth. All Gurdwaras provide langar which is basically vegetarian food served from the Gurdwara kitchen for free. So why not visit a Gurdwara and enjoy the langar. Find out the local Gurdwara at your hotel.

Visit a Sikh temple – The Guru Gurdwara

Buy cheap stuff on the streets

Why not buy some cheap stuff on the streets of India. Most cities, towns and villages have markets and you will be able to buy almost anything. Some of the cheap things could include clothes, bangles and other jewellery, handicrafts, cheap hand bags and so on. You never know, you might find something useful. You can buy souvenirs for yourself or give to your friends back home. Here's a list of things to buy in India:
http://www.shalusharma.com/what-to-buy-in-india

You will find plenty of these stalls on the roadside. Why not buy some cheap stuff. You never know, you might like something

Have a Masala Dosa

Although this dish is South Indian, it is very popular all over India and most restaurants will serve it. The masala dosa is made of rice flour rolled like a pancake stuffed with potatoes and served with sambar (tentils) and coconut chutney. You won't find it in the Indian restaurants in the West unless it happens to be South India restaurant. If you like Indian food then you will like this dish. Don't go back home without trying the masala dosa.

The masala dosa

Get a cheap haircut

Treat yourself with a haircut in India. Haircuts in India are a lot cheaper than in the West so why not get yourself one. It will obviously depend on which shop you go to but you can always ask before you enter. There are street barbers as well and will cut and shave you at a very low price. Ladies could visit the numerous beauty parlours at the markets. You hotel should be able to direct you to a decent one.

A hair salon. Get your hair done at a fraction of the price

Ride an elephant

Riding an elephant is a lot of fun so why not take the opportunity and ride an elephant. Although it may be a little difficult to ride an elephant as you will have to find one. The best place would be a zoo but not all zoos allow you to ride the elephant. Certain places like the forest authorities of Thekkady and the Muthanga Wildlife Sanctuary in northern Kerala organises elephant rides. Some tourist places like the Amer Fort in Rajasthan will have elephant rides. In fact, there will be elephant rides up the mountain to the Amber Palace. They are designed the way the kings and maharajas use to ride elephants.

Ride an elephant in India

Go for a camel safari

If you have not ridden a camel before then this is something you must try. It's not an easy thing to do as it is very uncomfortable but if you get the hang of it, then it can be quite fun. Why not take a camel safari across the desert in Jaisalmer, Mandawa, Ajmer or Puskar in Rajasthan. It's definitely an experience you will cherish for the rest of your life. There are various types of camel safaris from half days to full days while some include overnight stay in tents.

Go on a camel safari

Smoke beedis

Those who smoke might like to try the Indian version of the cigarette called the beedis. We all know that smoking is bad for you but if you are a smoker then you are going to smoke so why not try something different. Beedis are basically leaves filled with tobacco flakes. They are very popular in the villages. You can think of beedis as the poor man's cigarettes. They are very cheap and you should be able to buy them in bundles for a few rupees.

Smoke beedis at your own risk

See burning dead bodies

This is for the spiritually inclined and it might seem unusual but it's a common site on the ghats or banks of the holy city of Varanasi. Bodies are burnt all year round on the ghats of Varanasi. Hindus cremate their dead in the open mostly on the banks of the river where the ashes are then scattered. If you take a boat ride along the River Ganges then you can't help seeing smoke from the funeral pyres.

The ghats of Vanarasi

Get henna tattoo

This is for the ladies! Henna is very popular amongst the girls and women in India. They are called Mehndi and form an integral pat of Indian culture particularly weddings and festivals. Why not get your hand painted with henna. The good thing is that henna tattoos are temporary and they will wash away after a while so why not get one. You will have to enquire at your hotel where to get it done. The local beauty parlour (salon) should be able to do it for you. They will show you a list of designs. You choose one and they will have it painted for you on the palm and/or back of the palm. Sometimes you will find henna artists sitting on the side of the roads who will be able to do the painting for you. You should easily find a henna artist; it's just a matter of looking around.

Get a henna tattoo

Attend an Indian wedding

If you can attend an India wedding then that will give you a lot of idea about Indian culture, religion and beliefs. Basically Indian weddings are very colourful and Indians love going to one. There is music, dance, religious ceremony and of course great food. Men, women and children wear their best clothes. Marriages in India are arranged and the idea is that the groom brings a party called a "baraat" to the girl's house and takes her away. The coming of the baarat is accompanied by music and dance, something that you will really like. The wedding is organised by the bride's father. If you can attend a Indian wedding, you will certainly have a lot of fun.

Traditional Indian music at a wedding

Eat Indian style chow mein

Though chow mein is a Chinese dish, it is very popular in India. There are lots of little outlets and stalls selling this dish. The funny this is that, the chow mein recipe has been slightly modified a bit to cater for the Indian palate. Therefore, you will realise that it's slightly hotter and has been spiced up a little with Indian spices. So if you love Chinese food then make sure to try the Indian styled chow mein. You will find both chicken and vegetable chow mein in most restaurants.

Vegetable chow mein

Final words

I would like to say thank you for buying this book. I hope I have given you a good list of things you can do in India. Remember India is about experiencing and enjoying. It's not going to be a relaxing get away but more like a hectic holiday and a life time experience. Some people love India and some don't. I hope you are the one who will love it and will come back for more.

If you want to book a holiday in India then you can get some good quotes here: http://www.shalusharma.com/tour-quotes.

You don't have to buy them but at least you will get an idea of the costs.

If you have any questions on any of these things to do list then feel free to contact me via my website http://shalusharma.com and I will try to get back to you.

Feel free to subscribe to my newsletter so that I provide deals and useful information on India.

http://www.shalusharma.com/subscribe

Thank and best wishes and enjoy India...

###

Other books you might like

You can find them listed on this website

http://www.shalusharma.net

Essential India Travel Guide: Travel Tips And Practical Information

India Travel Health Guide: Health Advice and Tips for Travelers to India

Travel Delhi: Places to Visit in Delhi

India Travel Survival Guide For Women

Essential Hindi Words And Phrases For Travelers To India

Hinduism For Kids: Beliefs And Practices

India For Kids: Amazing Facts About India

Hindi Language For Kids And Beginners: Speak Hindi Instantly

Real Ghost And Paranormal Stories From India

Printed in Great Britain
by Amazon